Have You Ever Loved a Man That Didn't Love You

Callie-Lee Kuhta

To order additional copies of this book, contact:
Xlibris
844-714-8691
www.Xlibris.com
Orders@Xlibris.com

ISBN: Softcover   978-1-4535-1267-8
        EBook   978-1-6698-3611-7

Print information available on the last page

Rev. date: 06/30/2022

ONE DAY I WENT OUT LOOKING
FOR THE PRINCE OF MY DREAM

ALONG THE WAY I FELL ON A ROCK

BREAKING BOTH MY LEGS AND LACERATING MY HANDS.

LOOKING UP AT THE SUN
I WAS BLINDED AND I STARTED TO
SHOUT UNTIL I HAD NO VOICE.

DID HE COME, I COULD NOT
TELL BECAUSE I DID NOT HEAR HIM
IF HE DID.

ONE DAY I WENT OUT LOOKING FOR
THE PRINCE OF MY DREAM . . . .

My love I have found you
For deep down in my heart
I know.
You came so gently into my
life and held me close.
I love you.

Hold me tight in your arms,
put your mouth on mine.

I will feed you all the love I have,
that you will never hunger
again.

You held me tight in your arms.
You kissed my mouth, I felt needed.

We spent time together, we laughed
together, we made love together.

You gave me reason to care.

You gave me reason to love you.

ALONG THE WAY I FELL ON A ROCK . . . .

Did you ever love a man who didn't
love you?
It is easy.
Believe me.
It's like seeing a candy on a counter and
only getting a very tiny piece.
Knowing that you will hunger for more,
but believing that is all your worth.

I stay home waiting for you to call
or knock at my door.

I neglect my friends and family,
Because I am waiting for you.

But you never come.

BREAKING BOTH MY LEGS AND LACERATING
MY HANDS . . . .

Was it a game you enjoyed to play?
You knew that I loved you and
needed you.

Did you want to see if you could make
someone bleed with pain?

Now you know you did, what more do
you want?

Have you forgotten that I need to be wanted?

I wanted to be important in your life.

Getting screwed isn't all I needed.

LOOKING UP AT THE SUN I WAS BLINDED . . . .

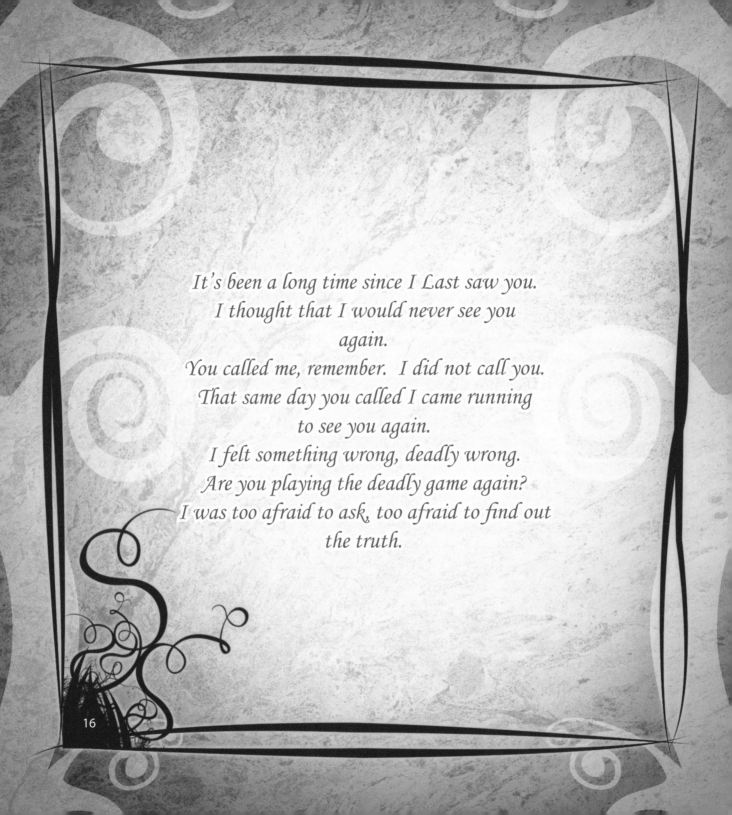

It's been a long time since I Last saw you.
I thought that I would never see you
again.
You called me, remember. I did not call you.
That same day you called I came running
to see you again.
I felt something wrong, deadly wrong.
Are you playing the deadly game again?
I was too afraid to ask, too afraid to find out
the truth.

You never spent any money on me.
You never took me out on a date.
You never let me meet your family or friends.
Were you ashamed of me, or was it you did
not want others to see what you are
really like?

Why did I let you do this to me?

AND I STARTED TO SHOUT UNTIL I HAD
NO VOICE . . . .

As time goes on, I realize that you
do not love me or care about me.

I realize you just needed me until
someone you could love came along.

I was just someone to tide you
over.

I know your life never centered around mine,
but I stood in the shadows.
Hoping, watching and waiting for you.

Maybe I cared too much.
Maybe I should not have given
everything I had.
Maybe I should not have begged you
to stay.
But I needed and loved you.

DID HE COME, I COULD NOT TELL
BECAUSE I DID NOT HEAR HIM IF
HE DID . . . .

Your phone was disconnected so I started
to worry. I went to your place because
I had to know, I had to find out.
I knocked at your door and the girl you
are living with answered the door.
I found out.
Was it worth the pain and sorrow to find
out the truth?

Did you lose your lover again?
Did you tell him not to touch you?
Did you protect yourself from the
Pain?
Did he hurt you badly?
You knew he was using you, why did
You let him?

Printed in the United States
by Baker & Taylor Publisher Services